# POOR
# WiDOW
# ME

# POOR

# WiDOW

# ME

Moments of feeling & dealing
& finding the funny along the way

# Carol Scibelli

PIGEON PRESS | MERRICK, NY

Pigeon Press
2005 Merrick Road #333
Merrick, New York 11566
www.PigeonPressBooks.com

First Edition

Printed in the United States of America

ISBN: 978-0-9832610-0-1 (paperback)
ISBN: 978-0-9832610-1-8 (eBook)
Library of Congress Control Number: 2011911379

Publishers Cataloging-in-Publication Data

Scibelli, Carol.
    Poor widow me : moments of feeling & dealing & finding the funny along the way / Carol Scibelli. -- 1st ed. -- Merrick, NY : Pigeon Press Books, c2011.

        p. ; cm.
        ISBN: 978-0-9832610-0-1 (pbk.) ; 978-0-9832610-1-8 (ebook)
    1. Widows--United States--Life skills guides. 2. Widows--United States--Biography. 3. Spouses--Death. I. Title.

    HQ1058.5.U5 S35                    2011 2011911379
    306.88/30973--dc23                 1108

Edited by Randi Cushnir
Book cover and text design by Dotti Albertine
Cover illustration by Gary Blehm

*In Loving Memory of my husband, James Scibelli,*
*and for our granddaughter, Skylar, who gives us all so much happiness.*

## Acknowledgments

Randi Cushnir—For your wisdom, creative approach, and care about every word. Your editing made an incredible difference, and to say I'm grateful doesn't come close to expressing all I'm feeling about you and the job you did.

Dotti Albertine and Ellen Reid—For all your terrific teamwork as my book designer and book consultant.

Jacki McQuade—For your good heart that has really helped our family pull together. You're a great daughter and mom, and such a strong, confident woman. And your expert eye for detail, talent, and smart solutions gave the book just the artistic touches it needed along the way. Thank you for dropping everything each time I called on you. I love you, and it's no wonder you were Daddy's favorite.

Douglas Scibelli—For putting up with my lame jokes, and calling you *Dougsie-Wougsie* for so many years. Thank you for asking me often how the book was coming along, and laughing the loudest when Skylar said, "Grandma, are you *still* working on *that*?" You're the kindest person I know (and very funny) and couldn't be a more sensitive son, always doing little things for me that mean so much. I love you, and it's no wonder you were Daddy's favorite.

Fanny Scibelli/aka Mama Scibelli/Nana/"Who's Going To Take Me?"—For encouraging my writing, and being my biggest fan in so many other ways, too, all these years. Most importantly, thank you for being a wonderful mother-in-law, and for treating me like a daughter. You really are my Mom.

Marion and Marcel Aronheim—For being my family and my friends all rolled into one. Your love and kindness can't be measured.

Carlo (Chuckie) Scibelli—For caring so much about the kids and me, and for being so sweet with Skylar. You have been a rock for me throughout these years, a shoulder to lean on. And laughing together has made these years easier, too. Thank you for reading various versions, for your honest feedback, and for giving me two of the classiest moments in the book.

Jon Rosen—For your creativity, enthusiasm and insightful input.

Robert (Roby) Scibelli—For reminding me early on that most people mean well.

Connie and Trifron Touris—For always being there for me and my kids, for loving Jimmy, for sharing our best days, and for choosing me as Alexandra's great-Godmother. A very, very special thank you.

Debbie and Henry Terranova—For all your help

these past five years. I don't know what my family and I would have done without you. I treasure your friendship, I love you and in all the ways that count, you really are my family.

Teri (Blondie) Schelin—For your loyalty and love, and for always insisting I look at the funny side.

Jade Yerganian—For your friendship and compassion, and for letting me know you understand by saying, "Everything comes with an oy."

Barbara Paskoff—For your amazing capacity to understand me when I don't understand myself, for encouraging me to keep one foot in the couples world, and for calling me a "stupid idiot" when I need to hear it.

Sheri and Fred Daniels—For many years of friendship, for loving Jimmy, and for being so aware that having you close by makes all the difference for me. Thank you, too, for those Sunday TV nights, just the three of us…even though Fred had no clue how to work the TV.

Michele LaFong—For our long friendship, for our many talks about the book, and for suggesting the Poor in front of the Widow Me.

Mickey Bayard—For being a continual cheerleader for me and my book (not in a girlie way, of course). Most of all, though, thank you for being a good man.

Carol Pack—For inspiring me to write more, and to write more often.

Vera and Jeff Wurst—For inviting me to every event and occasion you hosted (and for having one every 30 seconds); because of your graciousness, little by little I was able to walk into a room alone without feeling self-conscious.

Alan Querido—For being with me in such a gentle, loving way in the early days, calling so often, and sending gifts that sometimes made no sense to anyone but you. Though of course I knew it was my crazy, wonderful cousin's way of saying "I love you."

Dear Reader,

My life stopped on April 13, 2006. At 6:19 that evening Jimmy, my high school sweetheart and husband of 33 years, died of Burkitt's Lymphoma. He was sick for barely a month, and had just turned 56.

Our daughter and son were grown, and our little granddaughter was two. I worried, *Am I going to end up being the grandma in the back seat of the car?* But after some time, and a lot of bereavement therapy, I miraculously found myself eagerly anticipating my future more often than I lived in our past.

Along the way, I wrote down the small moments that had a big impact on me. Some of them brought me solace or, as I like to call it, grief relief. Others are moments that stayed with me because they each, somehow in their own way, captured the experience of widowhood.

As a comedy writer, I'm wired to be funny, so there's plenty to chuckle about here. Humor is honest, laughing is healing. And though these incidents are from my life, of course, I've come to see that the essence of my story is very much *every* widow's story.

This is what Jimmy said to me when he realized he wasn't going to live, "This will be a life-changer for you. It'll be an adventure." Often I say to him in death what I rarely said to him in life, "You were right, honey."

Carol Scibelli, July 2011

# Bargaining

As he lay in the hospital, I asked the nurse, "How does my husband seem to you?"

"Honey," she answered, "we're in ICU at Sloane-Kettering."

That's when I began stroking his face and making deals with him. "When you get better, I'll go to the beach with you all the time…Not *all* the time… Once in a while…maybe. I backtracked to tease him, thinking familiar banter might rouse him.

I also vowed to spend more time in Florida, the place he called "Paradise." I call it "hot and sticky and I'll take a snowstorm any day." That pledge I would have honored, though…in the winter.

I coaxed him to stay alive to disprove my theory that most people die within a month of their birthday.

On the morning of April 13th, 29 days after Jimmy turned 56, I pleaded with him to "wake up and live…You know how you hate it when I'm right."

Some people never get to say good-bye. I didn't get a chance to taunt him with an "I told you so."

He died that evening.

# Visiting Hours Are Over

"I'm sorry Mrs. Scibelli, your husband has passed," she said.

Images floated around me. Some of them I recognized as my daughter Jacki and my son Doug. We reached out to each other and sobbed.

Friends and family stood around in the hospital hall, not knowing what to do, or where to go.

Our vigil was over; after someone dies there's no more praying, or bargaining, or visiting.

So we hesitated, lingering by the elevator.

It opened, and out stepped a friend, holding a bouquet of flowers. I remember feeling sorry for him. He had walked into a minefield.

Much later I wondered what he did with those flowers, and if he ever brought flowers to a hospital again.

# Disbelief

After they told us that Jimmy was gone, like in a dream the scene magically shifted from the hospital. Now I was in a car clutching his pillow, feeling the cold metal part of the door handle against my arm. My head couldn't compute what had happened. Someone was driving, another was weeping.

How could the big, boisterous, intelligent man I relied on to make all major decisions succumb to a few tiny cancer cells, in four short weeks? My husband's life was over, and I was a widow, going home without him.

As I leaned my head on the windowpane, I thought of how Jimmy would joke with our kids… "When I'm an old man, if I feel myself going, I'll try to take your mother with me, so she won't live to be a burden to you."

There I was, at 55 years old, the burden in the back seat.

## Photos for the Funeral

I felt ancient, invisible and oddly detached watching my grown children play like six-year-olds on the carpet as they organized photos of Jimmy to display at his wake.

All I thought was, *Someday they'll be doing the same for me.*

# Blueberry Cake

had never been this close to death before. I'd imagined that a gut-wrenching loss of a spouse would be one continuous, dizzying carnival ride, making me so physically sick and emotionally spent until either I died too, or eventually came back to life as a smaller version of myself.

I've learned, though, we only offer grief a portion of ourselves, bits at a time.

People who lose other loved ones don't grieve continuously, either. We all seem to need grief relief to refuel.

The first time I witnessed this was the day before we buried Jimmy. My 40-year-old nephew Chuck, a man who never skipped a meal, sat in my living room, next to me. He and his uncle were extremely close, and he was crying, his hands covering his face.

My friend Sheri, who Chuck knew was an amazing baker, came over, and tried to console him.

"Oh Chuckie, I feel so terrible. What can I do? What can I do?"

He abruptly stopped crying, parted his fingers, and peeked out to say, "Blueberry cake?"

# I Lost My Husband and 3 Pounds

As I zipped up my black skirt the morning of the funeral, the material hung loosely and spun around my waist. I was thrilled to realize I must've lost some weight.

An instant later I turned to Jimmy's photo on the night table and apologized. I was alarmed to catch myself feeling happy about being thinner on the day I was burying my husband.

How could that have even entered my thoughts?

But maybe that's how grief is. Like labor pains, life steps in and lets us breathe…the reprieve between contractions.

# Seating Arrangements

There I was, his wife, his widow, sitting between our children in the first row, reserved for the closest of family; probably the only time in life people *don't want* the best seats in the house.

# Doug's Eulogy for His Dad

My father was my best friend. We talked every day. I would call him to talk about the horses, get his thoughts on the game this week. Maybe I'd pick his brain about the market, because he knew more than I will ever know.

A few times I would tell him about a cheap company I found that's gonna make us rich. He would say nicely, "You know, Doug, I don't know anything about them, but its stock is probably 30 cents for a reason."

We all know how funny he was. I'm sure we've all stolen some of his lines. If you've ever been to a Yankee game with him, you know he's the only guy who could get an entire section to crack up all game.

When my mother tells me I'm funny, I always say you know I get that from my father. That really bugs her, because anyone who spends 5 minutes with my mom knows all she wants to do is make you laugh. If she doesn't get you with her first 10 jokes, she will with the next 20.

My father was not a religious man. But he did believe in a higher being. And he said we all have an energy, and when our bodies stop, that energy moves on.

He is much needed here, but maybe some of that Big Jim energy was also needed somewhere else…

I miss him, and will make him proud.

# Ride To Cemetery

*Dear Jimmy,*

*Your cousin Lew made some calls and got the Southern State Parkway closed for our parade of cars to the cemetery. This was the first funeral for Doug's friend Jared, and he asked if they do that for everyone. At least it gave us a laugh, at poor Jared's expense.*

*We were riding in a limo directly behind the car carrying the flowers, with the huge racehorse arrangement John had made for you taking up the most space in it. But the only part that was visible to people driving by was the horse's head. So anyone looking over could've assumed it was a Mafia funeral.*

*I almost took a picture, but who does that?*

*We drove along, mostly in silence, and when I thought the kids weren't watching I looked up through the sunroof, and into the clouds, half-expecting to see you there, grinning.*

*Love forever,*

*Ca*

# Intimacy

Every night for the first few weeks I traced his body in my mind as I fell asleep. A beauty mark on his upper arm, the nick along his ear that I would play with in the car as he drove, the white moon on his thumbnail, and his gall bladder scar that blended with the one from his appendix operation.

Carrying these intimate pictures with me brought my grief to a rare place only another widow would know.

# Living Alone

The ice in the glass had melted, but it was still there on the kitchen table. Nothing moves if I don't move it.

# A New Shopping List

On my first trip to the grocery store after Jimmy's death I spent a ridiculous amount of time picking out ripe, but not too-ripe tomatoes.

I laid them in my cart. Then I remembered...I don't like tomatoes. Jimmy liked tomatoes.

## Thanks for Nothing

My friend's mom, who is 90 years old, became a widow at 60. She called me soon after Jimmy died, and right before we hung up she said, "You know, when David Letterman says something *really* funny I still turn to my husband's side of the bed and say out loud to him, 'That was a good one, eh, Larry?'"

I asked her, "Is this supposed to make me feel better?"

## Skylar Turns Two

Skylar's second birthday was a couple of weeks after "Pa" died. Jacki cancelled the party, and instead she, Glenn, Doug and I took her to the aquarium.

We moved slowly, trying to keep up with Skylar's pace and enthusiasm, but death had drained us.

After being entrenched in all things grief-related, to be out at a big public place was like walking from a dark movie theatre into a bright, sunny day.

The unofficial rulebook states: Survivors must keep his or her memory alive. But we weren't ready yet for playful comments like, "Daddy would be making fish faces now," or, "If Daddy was with us we would have had ice cream already." It was too soon.

So when I *did* make an attempt at a joke, saying that I only like fish on a bed of rice, I was surprised at myself, and even more surprised that they all chuckled.

This must be how grief works…our personalities peek out, no matter what.

## Moment to Moment

One moment I'm breathing normally as I sip my morning coffee. I look around the kitchen. "I can do this. I can be alone."

Then that icy panic surges through me. I call out to Jimmy, "I don't know how to do anything!"

He should have explained stuff to me. He never really sat down with me. He sort of tried. It was boring. I waved him away.

I begin to cry. It's *my* fault. I stop abruptly. No, it's *his* fault. He should have *made* me listen.

It's *nobody's* fault. We weren't living as if he was about to die. He was only 56.

# NOW...

Fear is all around me. Friends and family watched Jimmy disappear within a month. How can they not be shaken up?

My cousin Marion called today to tell me she and her husband Marcel have decided to take that trip to Italy, now. The now, of course, is "before some horrible disease creeps into our seemingly healthy bodies and puts an end to us."

My husband's influence on people throughout his lifetime was big. Now it's huge.

I wish Jimmy could see his loved ones today. They not only spend more money on themselves, but they buy *me* dinner. They offer to take *me* to a Broadway show. Who are these people? I always loved them, but now they're actually *lovable*.

The same people who laughed at doctor-goers are now making appointments for full body scans. A freckle that was always there now looks suspicious.

Couples married for more than 25 years buy new towels for newlyweds, and joke about needing a bridal shower of their own. Now we throw out our old towels and sheets and restock the linen closet. Who's more important than us?

Even my 88-year-old mother-in-law Fanny, who always *steals* SWEET 'N LOW from restaurants, and is famous for the line, "You mean you can *buy* SWEET 'N LOW," broke down and bought a box.

And my friends who were on a continual diet now suggest "going out for ice cream."

My world, my small circle, feels a little like so many did in the months following September 11th. We now know we're fragile, and we're scared.

It hurts, but Jimmy dying helped us live.

## Casseroles & Cleavage

Men have it easier. If *I* had died, women would be knocking each other over to bring my husband casseroles and cleavage.

And joining a grief support group would have made him *extra* popular. He wouldn't have had to move to Florida for 9-1 odds.

He would have been a good catch, too. I know. I broke him in. And to make himself more marketable, I bet that son-of-a-gun would've grown the mustache I always begged him to.

## Do I Sense Him in the House?

"Do you sense him in the house?" Gary asked me, cautiously, but loud enough for everyone in the room to hear. All other conversations stopped abruptly, like a train's brakes screeching to a halt.

I shifted in my seat and sipped my wine, slowly. "No, not really. I talk to the air, assuming he's there, and he'll hear me."

"I wonder if he follows you. Maybe he's here with us right now," Gary said.

I didn't share this with the gang, but I'm pretty sure if Jimmy was going to show up, it would be when I'm naked.

# Circling Widow

In the doctor's waiting room, while filling out a form, I look up to see a man and a woman holding hands.

I look back down to read where it asks "marital status." My heart jumps and my hand hesitates. I circle widow.

Then I glance up again, and the couple is arguing. I squash the urge to tell them whatever it is, let it go.

I don't want to be that weirdo widow who lectures strangers in the waiting room.

And would Jimmy and I have listened if some widow in a waiting room lectured *us*?...

# He Gave Up Meat...Was that a Sign?

Out of nowhere Jimmy gave up meat six months before he died. And I keep asking myself if I missed the signs...

Our grown son Doug was home enjoying an uneventful dinner with us when Jimmy tossed his lamb chop in his plate and announced, "Ugh! These are so greasy! I'm never having meat again!"

It's important to mention that Jimmy had a way

of making sweeping statements. After not having sex for three days, he'd say, "I guess we're never having sex again."

If a week went by without seeing our granddaughter, he'd sadly assume, "It looks like Jacki and Glenn are never going to bring Skylar here again."

Doug and I rolled our eyes, knowing his habit (though Doug *didn't* know about the "never having sex again" announcements).

At the time, I saw this "never having meat again" proclamation as just a quirky phase, like his *cowboy period*, where for about two months he only wore plaid shirts, jeans, a cowboy hat and a bronze belt buckle that spelled out JIM. We live in a New York suburb. Need I say more?

"Lamb chops are greasy, that's how they are." I shrugged, and kept right on eating.

"I don't care. Meat and I are done." Jimmy declared dramatically, like he was James McGreevy announcing he was "a gay American."

Doug laughed, and goaded him. "So Dad, when you're at a party and they bring around pigs in a blanket, you're not going to have any? You live for those."

"Nope."

Doug continued, "How about in the summer when we have a barbeque? You're not going to have a steak?"

"Nope again. My meat days are over, son."

Five months later doctors found a mass in Jimmy's pancreas, which must have been affecting his taste buds, and digestion.

We were so ignorant then, so cavalier…Nothing bad could happen to us.

## Our Family, Minus One

Suddenly our family minus one is grieving. At the circus, or the zoo, without Jimmy we are four empty souls slugging along, with each day floating into the next.

I can't grasp that my husband no longer exists, and that he isn't with us, experiencing the pain of loss, too.

I realize this makes no sense. If he were here, we wouldn't be grieving. I'm just not used to feeling anything so intense without him.

# Out of the Closet

I just came out of the closet. I'm not gay. When I need to be with Jimmy, I sit on the floor of our clothes closet. Here, surrounded by his shirts, slacks, and shoes, I try to feel him around me.

Visiting in the closet is more personal than going to the cemetery, and I don't have to stop for flowers.

I ask him things…Can he hear my thoughts? Is he in heaven? Does he know my future? Our children's future? Does he know when the world is going to end? Is he sick of me asking him so many questions?

# Running Away
# From Neighborhood People

For the first couple of months, as I did neighborhood errands, I was fearful I'd run into people I knew. Sometimes I'd pretend I didn't see them. Other times I ran away, panicked that if they hadn't heard my husband had died I'd have to tell them, then worry about *their* reaction.

Once when someone asked how he was, to fend off a long, suffocating hug, I almost answered "fine."

# Yapping and Napping

Practically all day long those first few months I had a running conversation in my head with Jimmy, and when I was alone, out loud, too. I found myself telling him every little thing I was doing and feeling. I only stopped chattering to him when I was asleep. I'd doze off and we'd both rest in peace.

This was not that different from our marriage. I like to talk, and Jimmy liked to nap. So it's probably no coincidence he started his napping as I began yapping.

But who knows, maybe now he's a better listener. He's got no baseball, basketball or football games to distract him.

# Caller ID

Not only did I run away from neighborhood people early on, but I also avoided friends and relatives who called me.

In fact, the closer the friend, the harder it was for me to talk with them.

How was I supposed to respond to, "How are you?"

It was impossible to explain, without sounding schizophrenic, that the only predictable and consistent thing about my mood was that it was unpredictable and inconsistent.

So I only answered when Caller ID said it was from Jacki or Doug. For all other calls, I'd stand in front of the answering machine, numbly listening to messages like, "Hello? Ca? Pick up. I just want to hear your voice. I know you're screening, but it's me."

"It's you I'm screening *from*," was my answer to the machine.

And turned out, silly as it may sound, ducking them was a win-win way to deal with loss. They got credit for reaching out to me, and neither of us had to awkwardly dance around what we should or shouldn't say.

# Clueless About Money

For 33 years I was smart enough to have a smart husband. I coasted through life without a clue about finance.

I'd joke:
*Does a spreadsheet have a thread count?*
*Is a hedge fund in the chipmunk family?*
*Do homeless people live in tax shelters?*

Now, life has whacked me on my head, and I have to use it.

# Bills to Pay

I'm fortunate to have Jimmy's assistant Rae, who for thirteen years made sure his office hummed, and it wasn't from the fluorescent fixtures; in crackerjack time she could put her hands on correspondence from 1994.

Now, Rae's content to carry on for me, but I'm afraid if I keep depending on her I'll never move forward on my own. However, I continue to flip-flop about it, because it'd be so easy to snuggle up with her, sucking my thumb, to block out the world.

The world snuck in this weekend, though, when Doug came home and noticed a pile of bills stacked on the kitchen counter.

"What's all this?" he asked.

"A bunch of bills I'm giving to Rae to pay," I told him.

"Come on, Mom. You can't pay your own bills?"

That did it. He embarrassed me. I have to expect more from myself. My son does.

# One More Time

A few months after Jimmy's death, our nephew Chuck was in my kitchen, reminiscing.

"I keep thinking about how Uncle Jimmy would sit right here, and I couldn't pass his chair without him expecting a massage. I would stop and give him a back rub, though I didn't always want to. But he was pretty demanding. Now, if I could do it one more time…"

I thought to myself, *I know what he means. I feel the same way about the blow jobs.*

## I Couldn't Say the word "Died"

For quite some time I avoided *saying* the *word* "died." Instead I said:

"He passed away."

"I lost him."

"He's gone."

I even toyed— once—with, "He's not home right now."

## I'm Still Here

I joined a bereavement group at three months. We sat in a circle and I kept my head down, to avoid eye contact with the other widows. That's when I noticed everyone was wearing ugly shoes. *Yes,* I thought, *I'm still here! Bitchy me criticizing people's footwear.*

# Trust

had an appointment with a private investigator. I needed to find out if Jimmy's partner John was honest, and figured having a PI on the case would be the best way to either alleviate or confirm my suspicions.

Bill, who I called Columbo, until he asked me to please stop it, explained that he doesn't do all the fancy wiretapping and cool spy stuff we see on CSI. He simply comes in as an outside accountant.

"Accountant? I'm thinking James Bond, and you're suggesting Mr. Rogers?...Does this mean there won't be a camouflaged van with one black guy and one white guy inside, both wearing headphones and stuffing their faces with hot dogs and cold coffee, saying, while they're waiting to nab John, 'That Carol sure is an idiot; the cash is in the…'"

Bill laughed, and we compromised. I hired him when he promised to emphasize the word f-o-r-e-n-s-i-c in front of accountant. It seemed to add a much-needed espionage feel.

I also hoped that as Bill got close to the books he might show me a little about how the business operated, so I wouldn't turn every conversation with John into an inquisition. I was tired of being ignorant and untrusting; finally I was a grown-up, forced to understand how the real world works, and it felt good.

If Jimmy was watching, he was probably thinking, *Is this my wife?*

P.S. Columbo cleared John. Apparently, all evidence was in my head.

# Is She Married?

I stare at women now and wonder if they're married. This is my new hobby. At Dunkin' Donuts today I stood in line behind a woman so bubbly I wanted to scream at her, "Stop it already!" If I'm not chipper, no one should be.

My instincts told me that she *was* married. She pointed to the Boston Crème, and her wedding band revealed itself. It taunted me, but I consoled myself with thinking, *At least her manicure is dull and lifeless.*

Can someone *look* married? The spring in her step, and her easy laughs, were clues.

I don't believe that married people are happier; I'm not delusional. Married people are lighter. Sharing the load of life frees them to bounce through the day, humming silly songs comfortably, knowing that at night their in-case-of-emergency person will be sleeping right next to them.

## Hearing His Voice

Several times a week during the first few months, sometimes even several times a day, I called Jimmy's cell phone, to hear his voice.

He was alive again for me in those seconds. And I may have continued to do this for who knows how long. But then one day I dialed, and all I heard was silence.

I learned later that Jimmy's partner had cancelled the account. It was time.

## Naming the Baby
## After Jimmy ~ Part I

My cousin Mark and his wife Seema were the first ones to ask me if I *minded* if they named their son after Jimmy.

"Of course not," I said. "It's an honor and a tremendous show of respect," I added. "Jimmy would be proud."

Often I find myself saying, "Jimmy would be…"

However, who really knows? Maybe he'd feel, *Don't name your smelly baby after me.*

Hearing Mark's intention was a surreal moment, because with few exceptions Jewish people name their babies after the dead. I hadn't quite grasped yet that Jimmy was gone. It had only been two months.

Then it turned out they meant James for the *middle* name.

I don't mean to be picky, but we all know a middle name is forgotten and unused as soon as the birth announcement goes out.

When the kid is five, and he's not cooperating, the parents might yell, "Andrew James! No more drinks of water! Just go to bed!"

Andy will know from their tone of voice that they're serious.

It's also likely he'll have no idea who Andrew James is.

## Naming the Baby
## After Jimmy ~ Part II

Mark's sister Judie had a baby girl and sort of named her after Jimmy, too. Her name? Liat Zoe.

What part of this says Jimmy?

Could it be a sibling rivalry thing? Just two

months ago Mark and Seema also pulled this. I'd better tell them none of them are in the will.

This is how it went with Judie…

I was staring at Liat Zoe, my second cousin twice removed, sleeping off the trauma of being born, when Judie summoned me to her hospital bed. I sat reluctantly. My emotional radar was on high alert. Anyone could say anything to me at anytime during those days that would bring me to a place I didn't want to be.

Judie held my hand like it was a delicate teacup, and she kept it for way too long. Then she officially crossed over my comfort zone by adding extended eye contact to the hand-holding.

Just being in a hospital where I spent Jimmy's last days was sucking up most of my strength. I worried that my response to Judie might be inappropriate.

And as I was busy worrying about *that, and* wondering when she was going to give me back my hand, Judie spoke. "I want you to know that we named our daughter after Jimmy."

I said what I say when I'm not sure what to say. I said, "I'm not sure what to say."

Judie seemed unaware that naming her baby Liat Zoe after James needed an explanation. She tilted her head the way dogs do when they're trying to comprehend, "Mommy will be back soon."

Finally Judie offered her reasoning. "Well, Brian and I always wanted Liat, and we'll call her Lottie, and so we thought we'd use a *J* for a *middle* name," she began.

"But we really didn't like any *J* names, and we love Zoe, which means *life*. Jimmy was so full of life. He loved life," she said.

A familiar feeling of grief rose in my chest, and then I chimed in. "Yes. Oh, yes, he was. He did."

When I got home I sat in my closet, among Jimmy's clothes, and told him the Zoe part was for him, because he loved life.

I imagined him responding, "I loved ice cream, too. Maybe some people should name their kid Rocky Road."

## Asking for Permission from a Dead Man

Mean Jean, my one-on-one grief counselor, was from the Snap-Out-of-It school of shrinks. I stayed because every so often she gave me a gem.

The other day she told me that when widows want to get remarried they often go to the cemetery to ask permission. I nodded my head. "I can understand that," I said.

Mean Jean lifted one eyebrow sarcastically. "Really?" she replied. "It makes sense to you to ask a dead man's permission for something?"

"Well, I figure that"…I stammered.

"Just for the record, none of the husbands ever say no."

# Why Am I Mad At Him?

"Why am I mad at him lately?" I asked Mean Jean.

"Why do YOU think you're mad at him?" she responded.

I ignored her typical therapist probing and continued to ask her questions I knew she wouldn't answer. "Why does it bother me so much that he never cleaned out the garage? Should that matter now? I'm a terrible person," I said, slumping farther down on the couch.

She didn't reassure me that I'm *not* a terrible person. She repeated, "Why do YOU think you're mad at him?"

Something inside me shifted. I sat up and told her that if he had cleaned out the garage, I wouldn't have to look at the white metal sides to my son's old bunk bed, the gray lacquer credenza from two houses ago and the ugly outdoor cushions that fit chairs which are long gone.

"I'm here alone with our memories," I said, my voice quivering. Then I shook off the emotion and replaced it with a sensible explanation. "There's no one to reminisce with me. I want to laugh with Jimmy about that disgusting lamp that Louis the decorator made us buy. No one else even remembers Louis." My voice trailed off the way it does when there is so much to feel and I can't breathe.

Mean Jean had the "it seems like we're getting somewhere" look. I told her I'm not going to ask her again why I'm focusing on the bad stuff. I already knew.

She baited me with a "Why?"

"There was so much of it, that's why!" I growled at her, feeling PMS-y, even though I hadn't had my period in five years.

She put down her coffee mug, took her feet off the ottoman and leaned towards me. "No," she said softly. "You're trying not to miss him so much."

## Lightening the Mood

Most people are shocked to hear that I'm a widow. Everyone basically says the same thing.

"He must have been young."

I tell them 56, and they gasp. Then some comment on how young *I* am.

I feel responsible to lighten the mood a bit, and today I found a response that did the trick.

"At least I'm young for something," I said, smiling. (The smile is key.) Immediately I saw their tension soften.

From now on, that's my line.

## Taking Control

I finally dealt with the huge pile of papers that had taken over my dining room table.

It looked like a crazy person lived here, and for weeks I either bypassed that room or circled the heap.

I would yell up to Jimmy, "How could you go and leave me with this mess?"

For a few insane minutes I'd even considered moving out, and giving the papers to the new owners, as a housewarming gift.

My solution was simpler: Two filing cabinets… the way for me to control the table (and eat off it, if I wanted to), instead of *it* controlling me.

Now it looks like a crazy, *organized* person lives here.

# Free to Marry

In high school Jimmy dated MaryAnn before he dated me. She never married. True or not, I always believed she was carrying a torch for him.

Today, a few months after Jimmy died, I saw her. At 55, she had just gotten married.

As we hugged, I couldn't resist saying, "So you waited until it was absolutely impossible, eh?"

# Lucky Me

I was born on July 7th, which is the seventh day of the seventh month, so I've always considered myself a lucky person.

During the first Breast Cancer Awareness Month after Jimmy died, I remembered what he often said. "As long as I'm alive, you don't have to worry about breast cancer. I'll take care of the girls."

That little phrase, "as long as I'm alive," echoed in my mind. I panicked and made a doctor's appointment. She was a new doctor, so I filled out some forms. Then she called me into her office to jot down my background information.

*Doc:* Are your parents still living?

*Me:* My father died when I was 17, from a brain tumor. He was 57.

*Doc:* How about your Mom?

*Me:* She's 81.

*Doc:* Is she in good health?

*Me:* Hard to say. She's mentally ill, and every time I call her she hangs up on me. We haven't seen each other in years.

*Doc:* Any siblings?

*Me:* My sister was three years older. She died when she was 50, of complications from Crohn's Disease.

Then the doctor looked down at the form I had just filled out. She studied it, and hesitated for a moment before looking back up.

*Doc:* I see you circled "widow."

*Me:* I sighed. Yeah, my husband died in April.

With a nervous laugh, she threw out her next question.

*Doc:* I'm almost afraid to ask, but do you have any children?
*Me:* Oh, yes, a son and a daughter. They're fine!

That was the moment I realized that *on paper* my life didn't look so lucky.

I'm like the lost dog poster: One ear, three legs, no tail. Answers to the name Lucky.

## Fender Bender

On my first birthday following Jimmy's death, I had a minor accident.

While I listened to Michael Bolton sing, *How Am I Supposed to Live Without You*, I sideswiped a parked car…a parked car.

In a heavy accent, the owner of the car I hit yelled at me. "Vat ver you dinking? Vat ver you dinking? Vat ver you dinking?"

I blurted out, "My husband passed away three months ago, and today's my birthday."

She continued to copy down my information, and without looking up said, "I hear what you say. Your husband he passed away, but mine is going to kill me!"

## Liberated Me

I'm looking at my overnight bag here in the closet. I need it for my two-day trip to Atlantic City this weekend. Last time I used it was this past New Year's Eve, with Jimmy of course, when we went to Atlantic City, with Barbara and Michael.

Casinos were our playground. Am I ready to hear the jingle-jangle of slot machines, and see men who look like Jimmy hunched over the craps table?

At roulette, a man will explode with a booming, "Yes!" and I will check if number 14, the number Jimmy always played, came in. Am I up for that? How will it feel?

The bigger question is guilt. Is it wrong that I'm eager to play blackjack again now without him?

Here I am, standing in the closet, waiting for his thumbs up. I state my case to him. "If I were the one who died, I'll bet *you* would have been back and forth to AC *lots* of times by now."

I promise him I won't bet more than I usually do. Immediately, I take it back. "Come on," I say. "You know I'm going to bet a little heavier without you to answer to.

"I have no one to answer to," I repeat aloud, more to me than to Jimmy.

So this is what liberation feels like. I'm liberated, all right, standing in the closet explaining myself to four rows of neatly folded sweaters.

## Blending In

I'm at the blackjack table, casually jiggling the chips in my hand. I'm comfortable here, relieved gambling can still be my enjoyment, my hobby.

Zipping over to a casino now and then isn't like dancing alone. Here people will assume my husband is at another table.

## Last Spouse Standing

In another 45 minutes it'll be the day that would have been our 34th anniversary.

Since we were married at 22, we *assumed* we'd easily make it to our 50th. We'd say, "How hard is it for us both to live to 72?" And we even figured out we could have a 75th anniversary if we were still around at 97.

How fun it would have been for the pair of us to be a burden to our kids. Talk about a payoff for parenting...Yet our last anniversary was our last anniversary.

Now, here I am, just four months since Jimmy died, *celebrating* alone. Our wedding song was the hopeful, "Our Day Will Come." How is it possible that our day has come, and gone?...

## Mausoleum Sounds So Grave

I bought the mausoleum next to Jimmy's, so eventually we can sleep together again.

But it's hard to visit him without imagining my name and date of death also chiseled in.

That blank square of terracotta marble beckons me. "Come closer. You're next," it taunts.

To make matters worse, my master bathroom is also terracotta marble.

Will I ever be able to take a nice shower again without wondering when it will be curtains for me?

## Dirty Old Widower

Today our grief support group *welcomed* a new member, a man who claimed he was put with the over-70 widows and widowers by mistake.

It was no mistake, or else losing his wife aged him a decade in the last three months. His adjustment to widowhood was remarkable. He hit on every woman in the room.

Sure, hook-ups in bereavement groups happen. But this guy thinks he's at Club Med.

Being a widow or widower doesn't disqualify you from being a dirtbag.

# The Old Folks & Me

The second group I joined met in the afternoon. I didn't think it through. Daytime attracts the elderly, like theatre matinees. Older folks no longer work, and they don't drive at night. They need something to do in between doctor appointments. My fellow group members were 150 years old.

As I sat and waited for the session to begin, these thoughts kept drifting into my head:

~ *Why did I let Linda drag me here? It's like I got on the bus to Atlantic City by mistake.*

~ *If Jimmy is watching, he's shaking his head and telling me to get out of here.*

~ *If I had died, Jimmy wouldn't be caught dead here. Yeah, caught dead…very funny.*

~ *Six months. How could it be six months?*

~ *What happened to outgoing me? That lady smiled at me. I'm not smiling back.*

~ *I don't belong in this club.*

~ *I should spit out my gum. Jacki says I chew like a cow.*

*~ Two men. Why are men alone so pathetic?*

*~ If I had died, Jimmy would be going to the cleaners and doing his own laundry. Then he'd realize it's no big deal…I really didn't take such good care of him. Yes, I did. I did. Oh God, I could have been more nurturing. But when he got pissy I just didn't want to please him. That's normal. It is.*

*~ That woman is kind of shaky. Could be nerves, or Parkinson's…No one looks too good here.*

*~ Well, I guess it doesn't matter what I'm wearing.*

## Too Old To Die

The husband of a member of our group was 90 when he died. She seemed shocked.

I repressed a laugh. Was it a nervous laugh or a mean laugh? Probably a little of both. They were married over 60 years—longer than Jimmy was alive.

I sat there and observed. At once her face revealed honest bewilderment beyond her grief. She truly expected him to live forever.

I imagine it's nearly impossible to accept that someone who has been in our lives for all of our lives isn't anymore, like when elderly parents die.

Maybe living forever begins to feel possible when someone has lived a really long life, riding the bumps, continually beating the odds along the way.

# Dead Man Talking

Group member Beverly told us she kept her husband's voice on her answering machine for months after he died.

So anyone who wanted to reach her heard a dead man saying, "I'm not home right now."

She couldn't understand why people had stopped calling.

# Long Illness=Time to Say Goodbye

Some group members said in a way they were grateful their husbands were sick for an extended time.

Invisible walls had built up over the years, and it took a terminal illness to break them down.

The time allowed them to say good-bye, restate their love and bring up subjects from which they'd previously run.

One woman said her husband apologized for not picking up his socks. Another told us her husband wished he had brought her flowers more often.

Jimmy and I didn't have that heart-to-heart. The possibility that he might die was never real to me; maybe not to him, either. I'll never know. But he *did* say to me he wished we had danced more often.

I didn't share that with the group. I wanted to. I couldn't get the words out.

# Three In A Row

Jacki sat across the aisle from me on the plane. I turned to her to tell her something, but she had already closed her eyes and plugged up her ears with her iPod. I felt dismissed, and though I knew that wasn't her intent, it still threw me into that vacant place where the air feels heavy.

I looked over at the seat next me and saw a woman my age resting her head on her husband's shoulder.

The only arm I had to rest on was the armrest, and I was sure all eyes were on poor widow me.

I stood to stretch, and scanned the rows of people, three across. A couple and an odd one were in each row. I used to be the couple. Now I'm the odd one.

Then I saw a row where no one seemed to know each other. I guess people *do* travel alone...

I just never thought about it before, like so many other things. Being cozily married had, in some ways, kept me insulated and smug.

Soon the sound of the engine preparing for take-off rattled Jacki awake.

She knew her dad and I always held hands during take-offs and landings. My wonderful, sensitive daughter reached over the aisle, for my hand.

# Family Vacation

A middle-aged couple near us on the beach asked me if we were on a family vacation.

My heart quickened and I blurted out, "Yes." Then, I thought to myself, *From now on this will be our family vacation. Just us…*

# Moving Forward/Looking Back

I'm writing this from Aruba. Jacki, Glenn and Doug are out exploring, while I'm hunched over my laptop, alert for any sound other than Skylar's rhythmic breathing.

Planning the vacation for all of us is new territory for me. I feel responsible to keep us moving forward, and I'm proud that I can do it. Yet, alone in this room, I'm acutely aware that I *really* am alone. And always on my mind is the thought that now we're making memories without Jimmy, leaving him behind.

# Everyone Wants to Help the Widow

All widows ought to have a posse as I do, men without motives who loved my husband.

Perhaps they imagined themselves as the deceased, and hoped *their* friends would be there for *their* widows.

That said, sometimes when they called to suggest something they wanted to do for me, in what seemed a way for them to also express their *own* grief, and sympathy, I felt like I was doing *them* a favor by letting them do *me* a favor. This is why I *allowed* Trifon, Jimmy's friend since they were five years old, to drive an hour-and-a-half from Jersey last Sunday, to clean up Jimmy's 1964 Avanti Studebaker.

Until then, it had been happily sitting in our garage, collecting so much dust I knew it was red only from memory, and that was fine with me.

A few hours later, though, that car sparkled. It gleamed. The car was definitely red.

But then the sun went away, and it began to sprinkle. I steered as Trifon and Doug, a man short, struggled to quickly push it back into the garage. (Jimmy may have been watching, and smiling, but for car-pushing purposes he was useless.)

Trifon then poured a thimbleful of gas into the tank, just enough so the Avanti would make it back into its old spot. And he soon headed home, glowing with pride; he had helped the widow.

Then later that evening I had to go down to the basement (now I proudly call it the playroom, since I jazzed it up for my granddaughter), and smelled something awful the instant I opened the door.

Afraid I'd be asphyxiated in my sleep, I rushed to find a 24-hour poison control office, and was waiting on the front steps in my flowered pajamas and white furry slippers when the fire truck, with lights twirling and siren blasting, pulled up to my house.

Five giants in firefighter gear jumped out and hurried inside. "Do you smell something funny?" I asked.

One whiff, and the biggest of the big said, "Are you kidding lady? It reeks."

Then they all went straight to the Avanti, gave a quick glance underneath it, and immediately pushed it out of the garage. Then pointed to the puddle of gasoline left in its wake, which looked alarmingly like a wet outline of a body at a crime scene.

Quickly, they covered it with white pads, to soak up whatever they could. Then all five men ran around the house, opening windows.

And one came down to the playroom, and looked all around when he said, "This is some basement, lady."

I was disappointed it wasn't clear to him it was a playroom, but let it slide. He was already busy setting up, and turning on, a huge fan he told me they use in fires, to get out the bad air, and pull in the good.

And soon they were gone, but not before asking if there was anything else they could do for me. Was there a place I could stay overnight?

I said I was fine, and I guess I will be. After all, I have my posse.

## Memorial Quilt

Doing the closet was easier once I decided to have a memory quilt made from my husband's clothes, for each of my kids. Squares of familiar shirts and pants would forever be on the foot of my son's bed, or the arm of my daughter's couch.

Not *my* bed or couch, though. I hadn't started dating yet, but knew at some point I would. No way I could imagine getting cozy with someone on the couch, having my late husband's entire wardrobe sitting next to us.

# Chat Room

As I wander through the message boards on line, I'm emotionally right there with most of the comments. This gives me a sense of community, something even my closest, well-meaning friends can't offer me.

Then it's revealed that many of these women have been widows for three, four and five *years*—compared to my three *months*.

My first thought is, *Some widows make the best of it, others the most of it*. And my respect for those in the second group plummets.

Then I catch myself. I hardly know anything about these people. Maybe after a smooth run their grief has resurfaced, triggered by a song, a smell, or possibly they watched an old video and saw their husbands moving about, talking, s*eeming* so full of life.

So they're stopping by the chat room for a booster shot, hoping to leave refueled, ready to face the world again.

And *whatever their reasons*, the more I think about it, their being here takes off some of the pressure I've been putting on myself to hurry up and heal already.

These veteran widows are "telling me" there is no timetable, no right way to grieve.

## The First Holiday

Being the self-appointed Matriarch of our clan, I made an executive decision for us to spend this first Thanksgiving with my best friend Connie, and her family. She and her husband Trifon are aunt and uncle to my kids; their daughters Kristi and Katharine are their cousins, and my Goddaughters.

Sharing Thanksgiving with old friends who knew and loved Jimmy turned out to be a safe, comforting way to get through this first holiday. "I'm thinking of him, too," was silently transmitted between us, and we felt he was there with us.

There was just a little more room at the table, and several leftover servings of apple pie, cannolis, cheesecake, linzer tarts, chocolate chip cookies, marshmallow twists, and vanilla fudge ice cream.

## No one to Share a Memory With

This past weekend Doug dragged the outdoor furniture into the garage, to store it for the winter. And I did what I do best; point and delegate.

Doug's a wonderful son, kind and loving, and he takes direction well. He'll be a terrific husband to some young girl who won't be worthy of him.

As he arranged the furniture, I looked around the garage, stuffed with stuff we had saved since, as my mother-in-law Fanny says, "Central Park was a flower pot."

There was the beat-up credenza from two houses ago. It was a built-in, but Jimmy and I purposely ripped it out to spite the buyers. They were jerks. Admittedly, we acted like jerks, too, but *they* started it.

I couldn't remember what the incident was, and now I have no one to turn to and ask. I can't seem to get used to it all ending with me.

# In His Eyes

Jimmy would regularly tell me I was sexy. He must have had an image of me from 1972 stuck in his mind. Those were the days when I could still turn heads, not stomachs, in a two-piece bathing suit.

I'm beginning to realize if we had grown old together he would've kept me young, helping me lie to myself longer, because I would have continued to see me through *his* eyes.

Now, without him as my mirror, I won't be old and sexy. I'll just be old. I can't take being desired for granted anymore; let's face it, new guy will meet me when I'm way past my prime.

Thankfully, though, an incident just popped into my head that helps squash that fear.

My cousin Marion married Marcel when they were in their early sixties. As Marcel watched the women in their 55-and-older community walk by one afternoon, he turned to a friend and said, "Why does every lady here *except for my wife* look like my grandmother?"

There it is. Jimmy wasn't telling me I was hot. He was saying, "I love you."

So now *all* I have to do is remain my lovable self, and down the road meet a man who appreciates my *mature qualities*, and can laugh with me at the benefits of a push-up bra.

## Too Soon To Date

*Dear Jimmy,*

*It's crazy that I keep feeling all this pressure to date already. I'm not ready. I miss us holding each other. But to be in someone else's arms? A stranger? I guess by then he wouldn't be a stranger. He wouldn't be you, though.*

*I wonder if you would be dating yet if I had died. Where would you find the women? Would our friends be fixing you up?*

*And what do I know about dating? Maybe I should have cheated on you, so I'd have some experience. Bad planning on my part, eh?*

*Then last night I was at the Friars Club, and Frank pulled me aside to press a business card in my hand.*

*"From one of the members," he explained. "A nice man. Very formidable." Said he could take me out, show me some fun.*

*Then he put his arms around me, told me I was a good wife, but you're gone now, and I'm still young and vivacious.*

*His eyes twinkled, and mine filled with tears.*

*I told him it's not even a year yet, but that didn't seem to matter to him.*

*Wouldn't you think that Frank, an old world Italian man, would expect me to wear black and keep my hair in a bun for the rest of my life, like Aunt Josephine?*

*What's wrong with me? Even Frank expects me to be dating.*

*Is this what you meant when you said my life would be an adventure?*

*Buying clothes at Bloomingdales, and having to sneak them by you, was enough of an adventure for me.*

*How do people jump from one relationship to another? I hear a song and still feel us dancing…33 years…together…It's too soon. You're still too close. Someday…*

*Love Forever,*

*Ca*

## Mean Jean's Thoughts on Widowers

"It seems like the entire tri-state area is asking me if I've started to date," I said.

Mean Jean responded with a snort. "If you were a man, you'd be remarried already, or certainly on your way."

"I know," I answered. "On average men remarry at two years and women at five."

"Do you know why that is?" she asked.

"Why?"

"Because men are babies." Mean Jean gave me that huge grin where she shows all of her teeth. I made a mental note to make a dentist appointment.

I've known her for months now, so I'm almost positive her bark is bigger than her bite. That gives me the courage to volley back to her. "Men are babies, you say. Is that professionally speaking?"

"Actually yes, it is. Been doing this for 25 years now, and I'm thinking of writing a book when I retire. I already have the title. 'Don't Flatter Yourselves, Ladies…Men Just Can't Be Alone'".

# 18 Again

I would have told Mean Jean she was out of her mind, if I had the nerve. Instead, I challenged her, as much as I dared. "How can you say that...that when I start to date *I'll behave like I'm 18 again?*"

"Because it's true. You will. You'll pick up where you left off when you were *last* dating."

Her matter-of-fact tone was infuriating. "Come

on, I'm 56 years old. I've been in the world, interacting all this time. I know how to be with people."

She threw back her head, laughing, and may as well have patted me on mine.

*How could that be,* I thought, m*y own therapist laughing at me. How am I supposed to respond to that?...Whoa. Wait a minute. Now I see why she said what she did. I haven't explained myself well enough to her yet...This ought to do it...*

"So, let me get this straight. You're saying my personality counts for nothing...Well, I know for a fact that most people think I'm funny."

"Apples and oranges, sweetie-pie, when it comes to seducing and being seduced. Flirting's an art...And did you ever stop to think that when a man says he's looking for a woman with a sense of humor, he might mean someone to laugh at his jokes?"

I had to smile at that, but it was *all* I could do, as my heart was racing. Everything she was saying had suddenly clicked in, as the session was thankfully ending. And I wasn't so sure she was wrong anymore.

I was halfway out the door when she called out to me, "Maybe this will help, Carol. Plenty of people *never* figure it out. They *never* learn how to flirt."

I didn't turn around.

And as soon as I got home, I Googled "How to Flirt."

## Dating? What Will My Kids Say?

Doug and I were talking about soul mates. He said, "I don't believe that people have just one soul mate, only one love of their life—except for *you*."

## Do I Have a W Stamped on My Forehead?

I drove to Atlantic City for the day. I went with George and June, an old married couple, and my good friend Marty, who Jimmy and I have known for twenty years. Am I spelling out p-l-a-t-o-n-i-c loudly enough?

What do four old Jews do when they walk into a casino at noon? They head straight for the buffet. You'd think we were being executed in the morning the way we piled up our plates. We dug in, it got quiet, and my mind began to wander.

*What am I doing here? I shouldn't have said yes. I wanted to come, though. But now it feels strange. Jimmy would have gotten the omelet. Then he would have gone back for more fattening stuff. "Hey, we're on vacation," he'd say.*

"Marty, I'm going back for another muffin. Jimmy and I used to pig out and say, 'Hey, we're on vacation.'"

*Am I talking too much about Jimmy? I don't think I brought enough money.*

"Marty, I don't think I brought enough money... Oh yeah, you're right, there's always the ATM machine."

*Jimmy would have said I <u>did</u> bring enough. Everyone took care of themselves, but Jimmy always brought a surprise back for the table.*

*Oh, no...there are the people who stroll around and play music. I hate that. A request? Yes, Go away!*

*The flute is right in my face. The guitar player is looking at me with pity. It's like the comment on my blog that widows have a big W stamped on our foreheads.*

*Wait a second. The guitar guy sees us as two couples. He doesn't know. Wow. Maybe when I see people giving me that look, they're not.*

*That feeling of being a fifth wheel—I know now where it's coming from.*

*It's coming from me.*

# Mystery Solved

Right before Jimmy got sick we were on vacation in Florida for a few days. He came back from picking up Italian food and said, "You have to sneak over to the restaurant and peek in the window. There's a lady in there who was so friendly to me, knows all about our family, and I just kept nodding. I have no idea who she is."

I laughed because this happened to him a lot. I intended to go, got lazy and didn't.

Then a year-and-a-half later I was walking my dog and a neighbor I hardly knew, who was standing in front of her house, waved me over.

I stopped and she said, "I am so sorry I never came by when your husband died. We were in Florida when it happened. In fact, I had seen him in Angelo's Restaurant down there and we had a nice chat. That must have been right before."

Mystery solved, but now that's another something I can't share with him.

# People Assume

~ If I look great, I feel great.

~ Divorce is the same as death.

~ A loss is a loss.

~ The man I'm with at the movies is my husband…oops.

~ I'm ready to date.

~ I want to date.

~ I'll never get married again.

~ Of course I'll get married again.

~ I'll sell the house.

~ I will never sell the house.

~ They know how I feel because their cat died.

## Sex & Jewelry

This evening I wore that stupid bracelet that's impossible to take off by myself.

Jimmy used to bargain with me. With a sly smile he'd say, "I'll help you, but how much is it worth to you?"

Some wives have sex to get jewelry. I had sex to get jewelry off.

## One Sink/Two Sinks

Of the thousands of exchanges between us, one suddenly jumped into my head when I least expected it.

Today I stood by the sink, brushing my teeth, and I saw my husband twenty years ago, emphatic and loud about not installing two sinks in the master bathroom.

"Every house on Long Island has a double sink in the master bathroom. It's pretentious," he said.

I gave in, and for years we fought over that one sink.

As this scenario played in my mind today, I couldn't resist looking up and saying out loud to him,

"Well, it took twenty years, but you were right about not needing two sinks, hon."

# An Ornament and No Christmas Tree

Two weeks before our first Christmas after Jimmy died the cemetery mailed me an ornament in the shape of a wreath. (I bet very few people know Pinelawn gives out Christmas presents.)

In the center, in gold, it read: "James Scibelli, 1950-2006."

That birth-dash-death date never fails to jolt me. I even find it upsetting when it's a stranger's epitaph. So the printed finality of it for my own husband was like a punch in the stomach.

Even so, I assumed the kids would expect to see it displayed. Though I couldn't imagine it dangling next to our little blinking Rudolph.

Luckily, I had a perfect excuse—no Christmas Tree.

Eventually, though, I decided to go ahead and reluctantly hang it over a framed picture of Jimmy.

The whole idea of the ornament was morbid to me, but I felt it would represent a respectful nod backwards as our family moved forward.

I discussed it with Mean Jean. She said, "You certainly expect a lot from a tiny holiday doodad."

Okay, maybe I *was* over-analyzing it, but the three of us were just finding our own style of grieving, and I didn't know yet if we matched.

I found out soon enough, when Jacki and Doug saw the ornament and *they* said, "Put that away. It's morbid."

*That* was a huge relief, but then unfortunately I had to go back to Mean Jean and hear, "See, you blew it way out of proportion. Like I keep telling you, you can't go wrong when it comes to your own grieving - if you just do what feels right to *you*."

## Our First Christmas Eve

We all claimed we forgot our cameras on Christmas Eve. Truth is we went out to dinner with our heads down, because no self-respecting Italian family dines out on Christmas Eve.

But needing some exposure to holiday cheer, we did, unknowingly choosing a restaurant that was off the charts in Christmas spirit. We may as well have been eating at The North Pole.

When the Carolers, decked out in brilliant red and green outfits, with cheeks so cheery they just begged for a slap, appeared at our table and began to sing, I rolled my eyes at Fanny, Jacki, Glenn and Doug, and reached for my steak knife, pretending to plunge it into either them or me.

Then Skylar squealed with joy.

I put the knife down. Her sweet little innocent face reminded us all this was new to her. She was only two-and-a-half.

She'll never get to experience the elaborate Christmas Eve dinners we traditionally hosted. She won't ever witness our friends and family shaking their heads in amazement at grandpa outdoing himself yet again. She will never be able to watch him proudly announce to our guests, "abbondanza!" (Italian for abundance.)

For the rest of the night, we struggled to stay in the moment for Sklyar, to make sure this lightweight Christmas Eve memory for us was as festive as possible for her.

Christmas Eve will never be abbondanza again, but next year I'll put up a tree, and we'll begin a new era of traditions.

# Tony Baloney

This ridiculously sweet little dog climbed into my lap, and fit perfectly. Still, I surprised myself when I hesitated to say, "I'll take him."

I had always wanted a dog, but when the kids were growing up Jimmy nixed my pleas to get one, using allergies as the lame excuse.

Now that it was poor widow me making decisions that no one vetoed, I had to ask myself if I really wanted the responsibility, and would be thrilled every day and night about rushing home to feed and walk him, no matter if it was eleven degrees outside.

"You said you might be ready for a new man in your life." my friend Sheri persisted. "And this Morkie needs a home."

Then she forced the face of the adorable Yorkie-Maltese mix into mine, like a pushy salesperson who thrusts an outfit at you, then spins you around to gawk at yourself in the mirror.

And as I held his head in both my hands, and smoothed back his silver and blonde fur, he licked my nose and stared right through me, until he found my heart. As if he knew I, too, had evolved into a new breed.

The first year fog had evaporated, the seasons had changed twice and I finally understood that this was my life now. My husband wasn't coming home.

*Yes*, I heard myself thinking then, *I __did__ want another something to love.*

And the instant Tony Baloney moved in, it was as though someone turned on the music again.

## Heard You Got a Dog...

"Good for you! Now you don't have to come home to an empty house."

"He sleeps with you? How sweet—On Jimmy's side of the bed?"

"Tony's so affectionate. You must miss that."

"Nothing like unconditional love. I'd trade in my husband for a puppy in a heartbeat."

"Great that you got a little dog. They live a long time."

You just can't make this stuff up.

## Taking Off My Wedding Ring

The other day my friend's six-year-old, who knew Jimmy very well, looked at my left hand and asked, "Is that a wedding ring?"

I nodded "yes", and she immediately responded. "Why are you wearing it? *You're not married!*"

A month or two ago I might have tried to explain to her what sentimental meant, or told her that I still *feel* married.

Instead, that night, as I sipped a glass of wine, I took my ring off, knowing I wouldn't be putting it on again.

1972-2006. We had a good run. But I wasn't married anymore.

## Oblivious

A year-and-a-half after Jimmy died I saw Vanessa Redgrave perform *A Year of Magical Thinking*, Joan Didion's memoir about her husband's sudden death.

One line in the play underscored to me how oblivious I was when Jimmy was in the hospital.

Redgrave was explaining that when the paramedics brought her husband to the hospital they assigned her a social worker instead of a doctor. She said, "If they give you a social worker, you know you're in trouble."

The audience roared, and I was stunned. *Oh, my God,* I thought, *they gave me a social worker.*

I could still vividly picture her…a 60-something woman with her hair in an upsweep, who looked oddly old-fashioned, like she stepped out of a *Life* Magazine from 1962.

That's why I remembered her—not for the significance that Joan Didion meant, and everyone else in the theatre seemed to get. In fact, after she introduced herself as my social worker, and invited me into her office, all I was thinking was, *Why is this woman with the weird hairdo talking to me? I just want to get back to Jimmy.*

Then, sitting in the theatre that night, with my head already in the hospital, I decided to *force myself to stay there* a little longer, and try to recall as much as I could about those last days with Jimmy; Mean Jean had often suggested I do that, but I guess before I wasn't ready to look.

That evening I expected the distance would give me more clarity. But instead I envisioned the time in the hospital in disjointed bits and pieces, just as I had lived them, mostly a blur of faces and unimaginable decisions constantly being thrown my way.

I stayed stuck, too, in that confused, foggy place months and months after Jimmy was gone.

*Going back* helped me appreciate how much clearer I am today. I missed a chunk of the play, but gained a new awareness of how time, good friends, and, I admit, my work with Mean Jean,  had brought me miles in a short but long 18 months.

Live theatre sure is inspiring, although this never would have happened at *Jersey Boys*.

## Wine, Cheese & Crackers

He brought the wine. I put out the cheese. I forgot to buy crackers.

Oh good, I found a box deep in the cabinet. New guy and I drank and nibbled.

All was fine. Until I realized the crackers were stale.

My next revelation was they were stale because they were two years old—from one of the funeral baskets. I psychically sent Jimmy a mortified, "I'm sorry."

◎ ◎ ◎

# Letting A New Man In

Tonight was different for me. Usually when I sit across the table from a date, I wonder the same thing all widows probably do.

*How would I feel if he were my late husband—if the impossible happened, and we were both alive and available? Would there be sparks? Would e-Harmony pair us?*

In my imagination, my date Jimmy is sexy and fun. The evening feels natural, aside from the very unnatural *he's dead* part.

This night, though, my fantasy is turned off, because I'm turned on. M, the man I am out with, is so charismatic, and genuine, and has the goofiest sense of humor I've ever known. We laugh continually, and are heavy *in like* right away.

We joke about not ordering the Death by Chocolate cake—how widows and widowers don't take those kinds of chances—and are comfortable enough with each other to fence with our forks, stabbing at the last crumbs of the Tiramisu. I notice how blue his eyes are. I never liked blue eyes on a man before.

I excuse myself to go to the Ladies Room. This time, however, I don't use it as a hide-out from dreary dates; I don't talk to myself in the mirror like I usually do, saying out loud, "What were you thinking? Just go home already."

This time I see I look happy, like I feel when I'm with Skylar.

I say to my face, "Wow, I think I might really like this guy." I see my eyes fill up with tears, and don't even want to go there, to all that I'm feeling.

I just check my teeth, reapply my lipstick, and wonder if I'm going to kiss him, and smudge it anyway.

Then, back at the table, I see that M, in an attempt to keep my coffee hot, has covered the cup with the saucer. The kind of thing Jimmy would do.

Yes, I'll definitely be kissing him tonight.

## Mr. Right at the Wrong Time?

After two months, spending Saturday nights with M was a given.

They say happily married people are eager to be a couple again, to be able to face the world as a pair.

That seemed true for me. He was such a good person, and we fit so well.

But in my house, surrounded by all things Jimmy, when he would call me baby it made my motor stop.

And often when I'd introduce him, I tripped over the word bbboyfriend.

By the time I met him, I had finally gotten comfortable going places and doing things on my own.

It used to feel scary and unnatural to not be able to *check in* with my husband. Now, having no one to answer to, felt freeing.

It was four o'clock Saturday afternoon when my cell phone rang.

"Hi," said M. "Where are you?"

"In the mall," I answered. "What are *you* doing?"

"I'm pacing the floor, baby, dying to come over and see you."

"Eight o'clock, right?" I asked, distracted by a price tag.

"Right," he replied. "I was just hoping to move it up a little."

"But the Spring Collection is out," I heard myself say.

Immediately, I knew that he was, too.

That night I told M that it wasn't him. It was poor widow me—after years of struggling to *uncouple*—opting, at least for now, to be alone.

# Making Plans/Breaking Plans

At Camp Widow, a conference in San Diego, a woman whose husband died eight months ago told me that the next day, when the event ended, she was going to rent a car, drive up the coast and stop at any Bed and Breakfast that appealed to her.

"What a great idea!" I said, thinking how brave she was.

But then a few hours later, when we were in group, and I told them her plan, she practically jumped out of her seat to correct me. "Oh, no, I'm not going to do that."

We laughed.

Most of us were widows for longer than two years, and we knew that common bereavement behavior is enthusiasm followed by panic. Something seems like a good idea at the time, and then *what was I thinking* creeps in, and wakes us up. In a flash, we take our toe out of the water.

"You all did this?" she asked.

Then she laughed, too.

# Growing Old Together

I just got back from the park, where I took Tony for a morning walk, and would've been home a lot sooner if I didn't spot this loving couple in their 80s throwing pieces of bread to the ducks over in a little pond.

I couldn't take my eyes off of them I felt so much envy. They got the time to grow old together that Jimmy and I never did.

I stopped walking. Just stood there, watching. Until Tony tugged on his leash, to let me know he was tired of waiting around, then began pulling me in their direction. Probably wanting to get closer to the ducks.

Soon I was face to face with the couple, straining to make small talk as they leaned over to pet him, oohing and aahing about how cute he was.

Then I did something I'd never done before with strangers. I blurted out what I was feeling…How nice it was for me to see what they had, since my husband died at 56, so we'll never get to celebrate our 50th or 60th.

Right away the woman caught my eye, reached out, touched my arm gently, and told me, "Actually, we just got married three years ago."

## Memorial Photo

On the first anniversary of Jimmy's death my kids and I chose a photo from just a few months before he died. We put it in Newsday's *In Memorial* section, and underneath we wrote how much we loved and missed him.

The second anniversary we ran the same photo with a similar sentiment.

When the third anniversary came around, I said, "We should use a more recent photo." Oh.

## Smelling Flowers with Grandpa

Wherever we all went together, Jimmy loved to carry Skylar from flower to flower, dipping her gently to smell each one. We remind her of this - so *we* won't forget.

## Dancing with a Stranger

For the longest time, whenever I 'd hear a slow song, I would feel myself dancing with my husband. I'd pet the hair on the back of his head, and our cheeks would touch. He'd be alive again as we glided along.

It's four years now, and Jimmy has faded from that scenario. As the music plays, I'm in the arms of a faceless man. Could this mean I'm ready to be swept away by a next love of my life?

## Thank You for Coming

The party's over—literally.

Last night I did what I never imagined I would. I threw myself a birthday party.

It might have been turning 60 that made me want to jump up and celebrate *something*. Life had been building slowly towards a throw-your-hat-in-the-air moment, where it and I could land firmly in the present, and stay there, at least for most of the time. I also felt I needed to release my friends and family, who had really stood by me during the four years since Jimmy died, and a party seemed to be the answer.

Both of us were born the same year, so I was sure if he were alive we would've had a joint 60th, and called it our 120th. We would have held hands while blowing out the candles on our cake, then raised a glass and made a funny toast, thanking everyone for being there.

But last night, of course, there *was* no Jimmy. So when the guests arrived, it was just Jacki and Doug planted like bodyguards on either side of me, and the three of us greeting them. About sixty people, one for each year, all seeming to come at the same time. The closest of the close friends and family; comfortable people, those who knew me best, the only ones I wanted there.

And, from a stranger's perspective, just observing, it might have appeared to be a jumping, happy, carefree gathering. But it wasn't. Amidst the drinking, and eating, and catching up, there was a subtle missing Jimmy feeling in the air; usually boisterous people were speaking softer than they normally did, the dancing was more restrained.

So I decided to interrupt the party, and aim to change the mood, by saying a few words similar to what I'd planned to nearer the end of the night.

I stopped the music, to get everyone's attention. Then, hoping I would be clear, appear strong, and not overly emotional, I began speaking.

I said I hoped they knew it wasn't just a happy birthday to me. It was also a thank you to all of them, for everything they'd done for me and my kids in the years since we lost Jimmy. I told them they really taught me how to be kind and considerate, by how they were with us. I also said I knew Jimmy would have loved the night, the food, the people. *And* the chance to make fun of me turning 60. Then I raised a glass, and asked everyone to join me in drinking to loving each other, being good to each other, and celebrating the happy moments—for as long as we could. Jimmy, I said, would always be with us, just in a different way.

From then on, the party took on a brand new energy; a heaviness was gone, expressions were lighter, movements more animated. Even the rain clouds parted, as if the sky brightening at last was a nod from Jimmy.

And once the house was quiet again, hours later, I reached over to Tony, whose tongue was working overtime, making the kitchen floor spotless for me, and scooped him up. I told him, as I slipped off his party bandana, that we did good, and were going to be okay. Then, holding him tight, I climbed up the stairs, got ready for bed, and turned out the lights.

www.PoorWidowMe.com
CarolScibelli@gmail.com